The Advent Alphabet

A Christmas storybook with crafts to make for every day of Advent

Anne Faulkner

Illustrated by Berni Georges and Jonathan Williams

Barnabas

An imprint of the Bible Reading Fellowship

Contents

Introduction

Most of us like getting ready for Christmas. There are so many exciting things to do at home, at school and at church.

Advent is the time when we try to think about Jesus coming as a small baby at Christmas and *The Advent Alphabet* is for you to use through the days of December as you get ready for Christmas Day. Each letter of the alphabet tells part of the Christmas story on a day of its own. Each day there is a short piece of the Bible for you to read and a decoration for you to make ready to hang on your Christmas tree. You might need to ask a grown up to help you make up the decorations each day, which will be a good way of preparing for Christmas together.

If you would rather make your own tree too, you can see how to do this on page 7. You will find the templates for the tree in the middle pages of the book.

Each day there is a prayer for you to use. You might like to use them as you hang your decorations on the tree. Or you could say the prayer at a convenient time of day—first thing in the morning or before you go to bed in the evening.

There is lots for you to do as you go from page to page and from letter to letter, but there is also lots to learn about how much God loves us all as you read this special story day by day.

Resources

You will find it useful to have to hand the things you'll need to make up the decorations as you work through the days of *The Advent Alphabet*.

For most of the activities you will need:

White card

Plain white paper

Glue

Scissors

Ruler

Pencil

Felt tipped pens, colouring crayons and/or paint

Thread (this could be thin ribbon, gold or silver embroidery thread, or various coloured wools)

A hole punch

For some of the activities you will need:

Glitter

Sticky shapes

Sticky tape

Fromage frais or yoghurt pots

Coloured crêpe paper or Christmas paper

Coloured tissue paper

Gold paper or silver cooking foil

A small amount of papier mâché, made with half water and half PVC glue, mixed together

For the Christmas tree you will need:

4 sheets of A2 size thick green card

Making your own tree

In the middle of the book you will find templates for the shapes needed to make an A2 size Christmas tree. If you make the tree before you start working through *The Advent Alphabet,* you will be able to hang each decoration on its branches as you go.

1 Carefully remove the four-page template from the centre of the book. Join the tree shapes together with sticky tape and trace onto each of the A2 size sheets of card.

2 Cut out and slot together as shown.

3 Secure along the length of each section with transparent sticky tape.

4 Arrange branches so that the tree stands securely on its base.

God sent the angel Gabriel to a town in Galilee named Nazareth. He had a message for a young woman promised in marriage to a man named Joseph, who was a descendant of King David. Her name was Mary. The angel came to her and said, 'Peace be with you! The Lord is with you and has greatly blessed you.'

Luke 1:26-27

is for the angel Gabriel

1 December

Do you like waiting? Waiting for your birthday to come or waiting for the first day of the holidays? How do you feel when you have to wait? Impatient? Excited? Most of us do not like waiting and want the time to pass quickly!

Before Jesus was born the Jewish people had been waiting for a very long time—years and years and years—for God to send a special leader who would set them free from being ruled by other nations.

They waited and waited. Some people waited patiently, but many were impatient and restless, wondering when God would rescue them.

And then God did something. He sent an angel to give Mary some good news.

We do not always know how God will act; all we can do is wait.

A prayer for you to use today
Thank you, dear God, for sending your angel to Mary. Please help us to be patient with other people and patient when we wait for you to answer our prayers. Amen.

Make this figure of the angel Gabriel.

1 Cut out the body shape and colour in.

2 Glue the card body shape at the tab to form a cone.

3 Cut out the two wing shapes and colour them in.

4 Cut out the head shape and colour in. Lay length of thread on inside at dotted line.

5 Fold on dotted line and run glue around inside edges of the head shape and hold together until stuck.

6 Slot the wings into the slits in the angel's body and glue. Glue the head in place.

7 Cut out halo shape and colour in. Slide over head at slit and glue to the back of the head.

Photocopy or trace this page onto thin card.

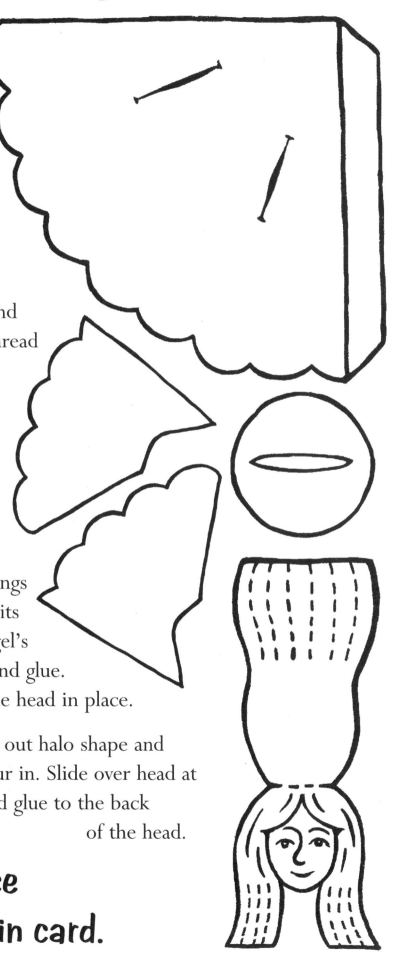

Joseph went from the town of Nazareth in Galilee to the town of Bethlehem in Judea, the birthplace of King David. Joseph went there because he was a descendant of David.

Luke 2:4

is for Bethlehem

2 December

Nowadays long journeys are not usually a problem for us. We catch a train, a bus or even a plane and we are used to travelling quickly. Many of our families have cars and so we do not even have to carry our luggage.

It was not nearly so easy for Joseph. Bethlehem was a special town, as king David had been born there a long time before, but the road between Nazareth and Bethlehem was long and sometimes dangerous. It took days of travelling, mostly walking, to make the journey.

Just imagine how pleased Joseph was when he saw the roof tops of Bethlehem in the distance and he knew that he was nearly there.

A prayer for you to use today

Dear Lord, thank you for all the things that we take for granted—like cars and trains. Thank you for special places in our lives. Amen

Make the bells of Bethlehem to remind you that it has been a special place for many hundreds of years.

1 Take two small bell-shaped *fromage frais* pots (make sure that they are clean).

2 Carefully trim round the square edges if they have come from a multipack.

3 Cover them completely with a thin layer of papier mâché made with small strips of paper and stuck with half water and half PVC glue, mixed together.

4 Leave to dry and then make a small hole in the base of each bell.

5 Paint your bells or decorate with coloured sticky shapes.

6 Thread ribbon or string through the holes and tie the bells together so that they will hang on your tree.

11

At that time the Emperor Augustus ordered a census to be taken throughout the Roman Empire. Everyone, then, went to register himself, each to his own town.

Luke 2:1–2

is for census

3 December

Can you imagine trying to count all the people in your town?. How do you think you could do it? It would not be very easy. These days we send people forms to fill in, but at the time of the Roman Emperor Augustus, people were told to return to the place of their birth. There they had to register there, even if they did not want to go. This was the reason why Joseph travelled all that way to Bethlehem, but *we* know that it was also because God wanted Joseph to be in Bethlehem.

God uses all kinds of situations to help people know about him, and we do not always understand what he is doing.

A prayer for you to use today

Dear God. Thank you that you know each of us by name and that you always want the best for us. Amen

Make a census cracker for your Christmas tree.

1 Cut the small rectangle out of card and glue to form a cylinder.

2 Using Christmas or crepe paper, cut out the large cracker cover.

3 Glue the paper cover round the small cylinder.

4 Gather each end of the cracker just below the card tube and tie with cotton to form the hanger.

5 Write the names of your friends (or your class at school or at church) on small pieces of paper and glue them on the outside of the cracker.

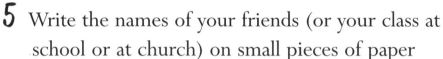

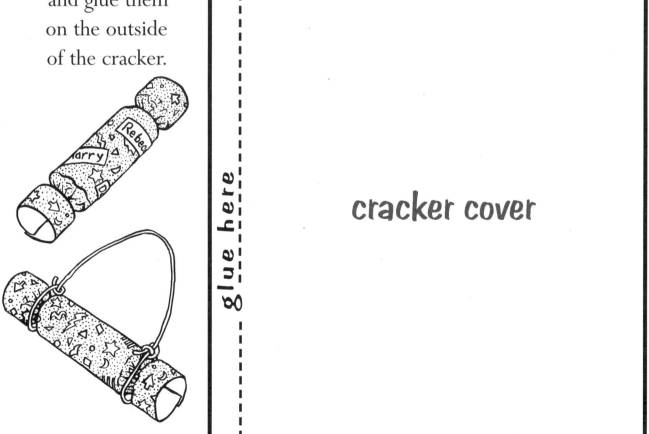

glue here

cracker cover

Photocopy or trace this page onto thin card.

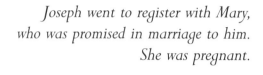

D is for donkey

4 December

Joseph went to register with Mary, who was promised in marriage to him. She was pregnant.

Luke 2:5

The donkey is not actually mentioned in this story in the Bible. Donkeys were a way that poorer people could travel without too much expense when they needed to go on a long journey. Donkeys are hard working, patient and reliable, and are capable of carrying heavy loads. It may well be that Joseph had a donkey for Mary to ride on, so that she did not get too tired. We do not really know, but we like the idea of the simple, gentle donkey carrying Mary. Perhaps you have sung the carol 'Little Donkey' which goes like this:

Little donkey, little donkey,
on a dusty road
got to keep on plodding onward
with your heavy load.

A prayer for you to use today
Loving God, today we thank you for the gentle donkey who made that journey to Bethlehem. We thank you for all animals, and especially for our pets. Help us to care for them properly. Amen.

Make a donkey for your tree.

1 Colour and cut out the pieces of the outline of the donkey.

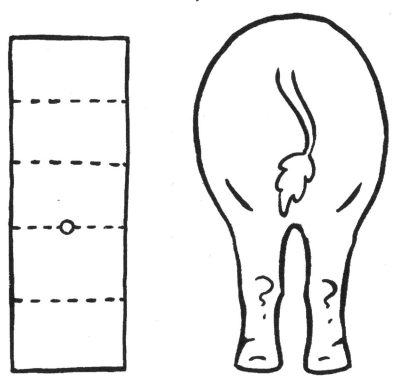

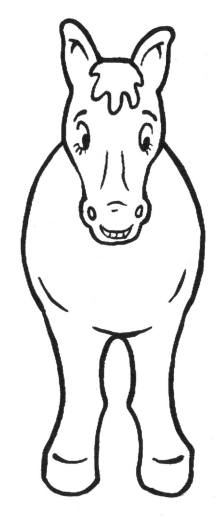

2 Cut out the strip and fold it as shown. Punch a hole where shown. Stick front and back of donkey to ends of concertina strip. Put 18 cm length of thread through hole to form hanger.

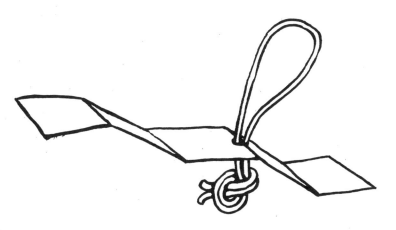

Photocopy or trace this page onto thin card.

15

Mary got ready and hurried off to a town in the hill country of Judea. She went into Zechariah's house and greeted Elizabeth.

Luke 1:39—40

E is for Elizabeth

5 December

It's really good to have a friend, a special friend who can share your secrets, cheer you up, and play with you. Do you ever stay with a friend or go on holiday together? Do you ever phone up your friends to tell them special news?

Mary had a special friend, who was her cousin Elizabeth. After the angel Gabriel had told Mary that she was to have a baby who would change the world, Mary was so excited that she rushed off to see Elizabeth and to share her secret. Elizabeth was very pleased too.

A prayer for you to use today

Our friends are very special to us. Thank you for them and for all the fun we have and the secrets we share. Amen.

Make the smiley face of Elizabeth.

1 Cut out the two head shapes, and draw your picture of Elizabeth's face on one piece. Colour it in—make sure that she is smiling.

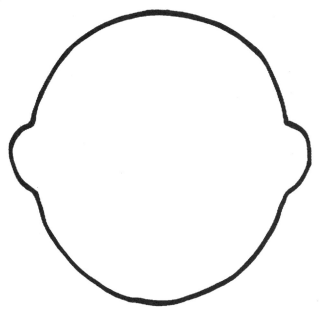

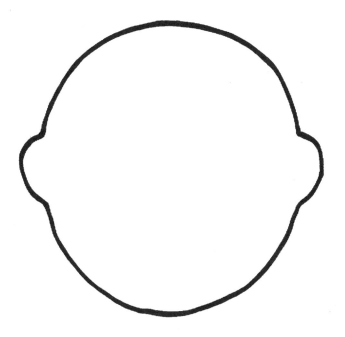

2 Colour the hair or glue wool or paper curls to the second piece.

3 Glue some ribbon or string on the back so that you can hang Elizabeth's smiley face on your tree.

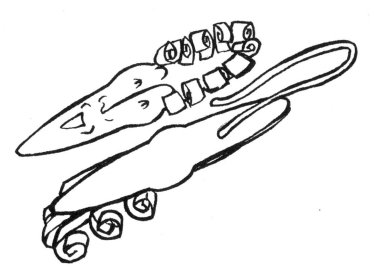

4 Glue the front and the back of the head together.

Photocopy or trace this page onto thin card.

F is for flocks

6 December

There were some shepherds in that part of the country who were spending the night in the fields, taking care of their flocks.

Luke 2:8

Sheep need looking after. Have you ever seen sheep in a field or on a hillside? The sheep in this part of the story were outside in the fields at night. The shepherds watched over them to make sure that they were safe from harm. The shepherds did not leave the sheep on their own at all.

Later on in the Bible, Jesus calls himself the Good Shepherd, because he cares for us and watches over us to keep us safe. Whatever we are doing he is near to us because he loves us.

A prayer for you to use today

Dear Lord Jesus, we thank you for always watching over us, even when we do not think about you. Amen.

Make these sheep for your tree.

1   Cut out the body shape for the sheep.

2   Colour the sheep if you want to
(Bethlehem sheep are not white,
more of a dirty brown colour).

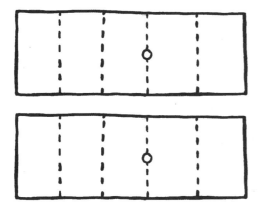

3   Cut out the strips and fold as shown.
Punch a hole where shown.
Stick front and back of sheep
to ends of concertina strip.
Put 18 cm length of thread
through hole to form hanger.

Photocopy or trace this page onto thin card.

An angel appeared to Joseph in a dream and said, 'Joseph, descendant of David, do not be afraid to take Mary to be your wife. She will have a son, and he will be called Immanuel, which means "God is with us".'

Matthew 1:20–21, 23

G is for God is with us

7 December

So this baby that the angel told Mary about, and who Mary told Elizabeth about, was to be a very special baby. He was described as *Immanuel*. He was a sign that God is with us, that God loves us.

It is hard for us to know how much God loves us, or for us to think about what he looks like. This is why he sent his Son, Jesus, as a baby who would grow up and live on earth.

Jesus was a wonderful gift to show that God is with us.

A prayer for you to use today

Father God, we know that you are always with us, but we sometimes find that hard to understand. Thank you for sending us your Son, Jesus, to be with us, and to help us know more about your love for us. Amen.

Make a dove to go on your Christmas tree.

Take a piece of paper 210 mm square.

1 Fold on diagonal AB.

2 Fold D back at EF.

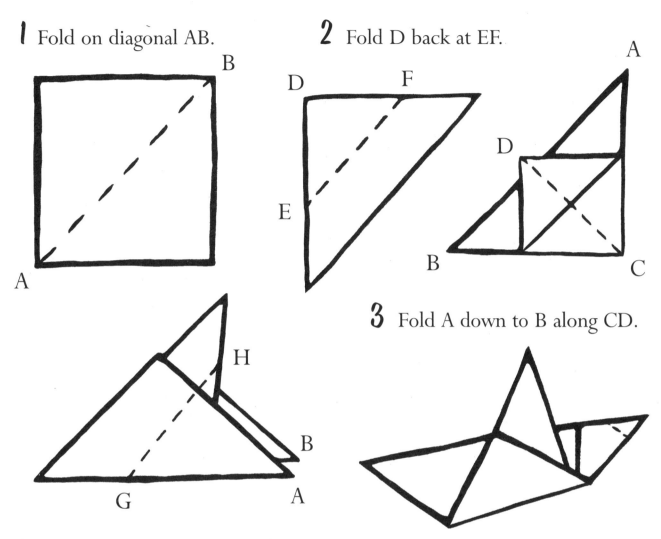

3 Fold A down to B along CD.

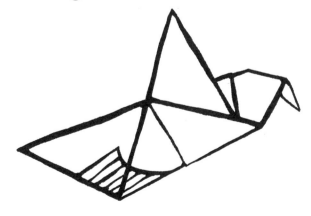

4 Fold A and B up at GH to form a wing on each side of the dove's body.

5 Fold top point down to form the dove's beak.

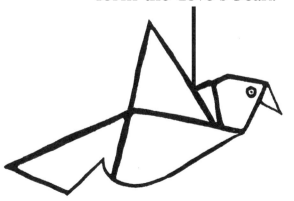

6 Cut shaded area away to form the tail and draw in the eyes.

7 Attach string or ribbon to your dove's back and hang it on the tree.

21

Jesus was born in the town of Bethlehem in Judea, during the time when Herod was king. When King Herod heard about this, he was very upset, and so was everyone else in Jerusalem. He called together all the chief priests and the teachers of the law and asked them, 'Where will the Messiah be born?'

Matthew 2:1, 3–4

L is for Herod

8 December

There are good, nice people in the world and there are people who are not very nice and who do unkind and horrid things. As we know, the Jewish people were hoping for a special leader to save them from the Romans. This leader would be the Messiah. The word Messiah means 'God's chosen one'; in other words —Jesus.

King Herod was not a very good or nice person. He pretended to be pleased to hear about this special baby who was expected, but he was cross and jealous and not really at all pleased.

A prayer for you to use today

Lord Jesus, we know that not everyone welcomes you at Christmas, or wants to know you. We pray for those who do not love you and those who do not want to please you. Amen.

Make the figure of King Herod to remind you that not everyone was pleased to welcome God's Son. This continued all through Jesus' life.

1 Cut out the main body parts of King Herod and colour them in. Cut out the cross face of Herod and colour it in. Make a slit along the dotted lines.

2 Stick a 17 cm length of thread on the back of one of the body pieces as shown to form a hanger.

3 Glue the two body parts together. Slip Herod's cross head over the figure—you'll have a cross face or a smiling face showing depending on which way you slip it over his head.

Photocopy or trace this page onto thin card.

I is for inn

While Mary and Joseph were in Bethlehem, the time came for her to have her baby. She gave birth to her first son, wrapped him in strips of cloth and laid him in a manger —there was no room for them to stay in the inn.

Luke 2:6–7

9 December

Do you have a comfortable, warm bedroom in your house? Do you have a soft bed, a carpet on the floor and curtains at the window?

When we welcome a new baby into the family, we often take a great deal of trouble to buy special things for him or her; like a cradle, a small blanket and soft toys.

When Mary and Joseph arrived in Bethlehem, maybe Mary was riding on the donkey, but they were both tired. There were so many people in Bethlehem because of the census that the inn where they had hoped to stay was full. There was nowhere for them to go, no special room, no special cradle or blanket for this baby when he came into the world.

A prayer for you to use today

Father God, it is easy for us to forget those who are not as comfortable as we are ourselves. We pray for your blessing upon those people who are homeless, in this country or abroad. Amen.

Make the flat-topped inn which would have been just like many of the houses in Bethlehem—even today.

1 Cut out the inn shape and colour it in.

2 Fold the inn as in the picture.

3 Fold the tabs on the marks and glue them into place.

4 Cut out the long rectangular shape.

5 Colour it in and fold it along the lines in the same way as you would a fan.

6 Glue the steps to the side of the inn as shown.

7 Make a small hole in the roof and insert a length of thread, knotting it on the inside, so that you can hang it on your tree.

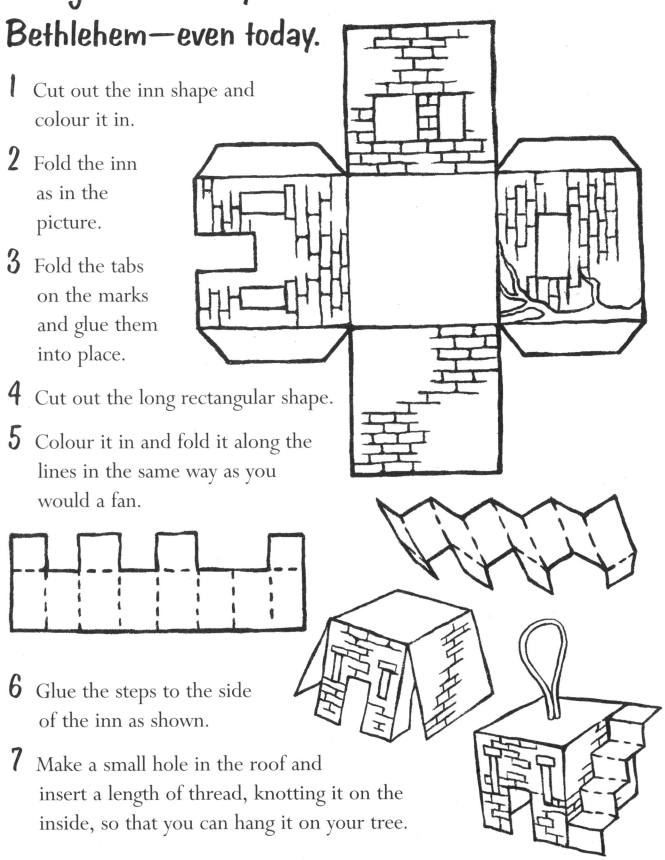

Photocopy or trace this page onto thin card.

J is for Joseph

*Joseph was a man who always did what was right...
he married Mary as the angel of the Lord had told him to do.*

Matthew 1:19, 24

10 December

How confusing and difficult it must have been for Joseph to be a good husband, and to obey what God was saying to him. He had to go on the long journey because of the census. It must have been very hard for him to discover that the inn was full when he and Mary arrived in Bethlehem. I think God must have known that Joseph was a very special person and that he would look after Mary as she waited for her new baby to be born, don't you?

Who are the special people who take care of you?

A prayer for you to use today

Dear Father God, you gave Joseph to Jesus to look after him and Mary. Thank you for all those who look after us at home and at school, especially...
Amen.

Make this figure of Joseph.

1 Cut out the body shape and colour it in.

2 Cut out the arms shapes and colour them in. Bend back on the dotted lines.

3 Glue the card body shape at the tab to form a cone.

4 Cut out the head shape. Colour it in. Lay a 30 cm length of thread on the inside at the dotted line.

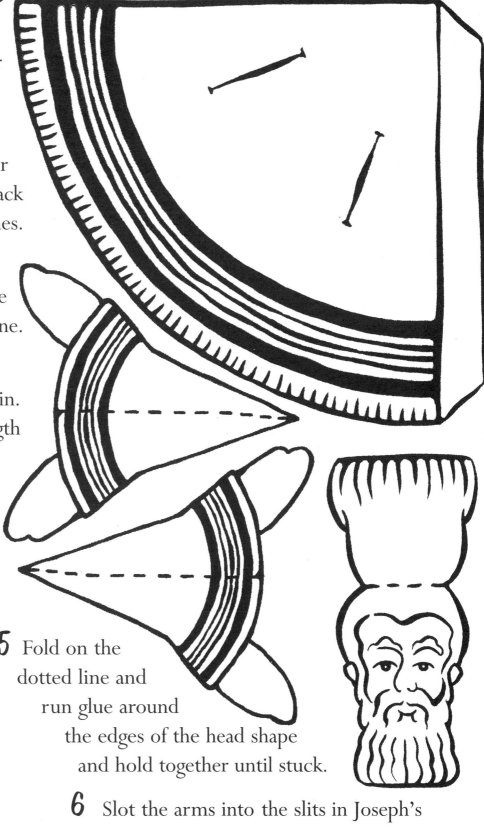

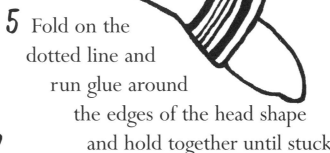

5 Fold on the dotted line and run glue around the edges of the head shape and hold together until stuck.

6 Slot the arms into the slits in Joseph's body and glue the head in place.

7 Tie the thread to make a hanger.

Photocopy or trace this page onto thin card.

Where is the baby born to be the king of the Jews?

Matthew 2:2

is for king of the Jews

11 December

This special baby, who we know was Jesus, seems to have different names to describe him. We have already heard how he has been called the Messiah, which means 'chosen by God', and Immanuel, which means 'God is with us'. Now he is being called the king of the Jews. This was because some of the Jewish people were hoping for a king who might lead them into battle and win their freedom from the Romans.

We know that Jesus came in peace and love. He did not fight a battle against the Romans, but came to tell us all about God. Because he is God's Son, Jesus knows how much God loves us—and he was prepared to come into the world and die to show us just how great God's love is.

Sometimes you may see the cross and the crown drawn together, so the front of the crown is a cross. This is to remind us that Jesus is our king and that he died for us.

A prayer for you to use today

Thank you dear God for sending Jesus in peace. Thank you that he came to show us how much you love us. Amen.

top of tree

join

here

bottom of tree

top of dot

here

Make a small crown.

1 Cut out the shape of the crown.

2 Decorate it with paint, coloured paper and glitter.

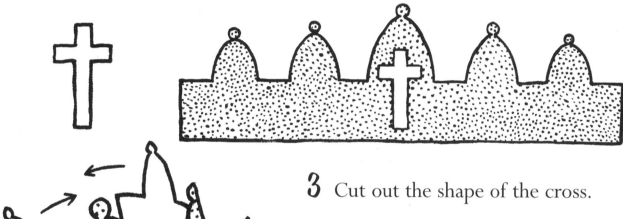

3 Cut out the shape of the cross.

4 Colour it so that it is clearly
different from the rest
of the crown.

5 Fix the cross on to the
front of the crown.

6 Glue the tab on the crown and
stick it in place.

7 Attach thread to hang the crown on your tree.

Photocopy or trace this page onto thin card.

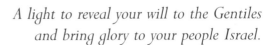

A light to reveal your will to the Gentiles
and bring glory to your people Israel.

Luke 2:32

is for light

12 December

In my family we always light the candles on our birthday cakes and then turn out the lights before the person whose birthday it is blows the candles out. Do you do that too? If you do, you will know that those tiny candles shine really brightly, especially if the room is dark. The glowing light makes everything look different and everyone smiles and is happy.

Jesus came like a light shining brightly in a world where people had lost hope. The birth of Jesus gave everyone the chance of joy and happiness, different from anything they had known before.

A prayer for you to use today

Father God, you sent Jesus to shine in our lives like a light shines in the dark, and to give us hope and joy. Thank you. Amen.

Make a candle for your Christmas tree to remind you that Jesus is the light of the world.

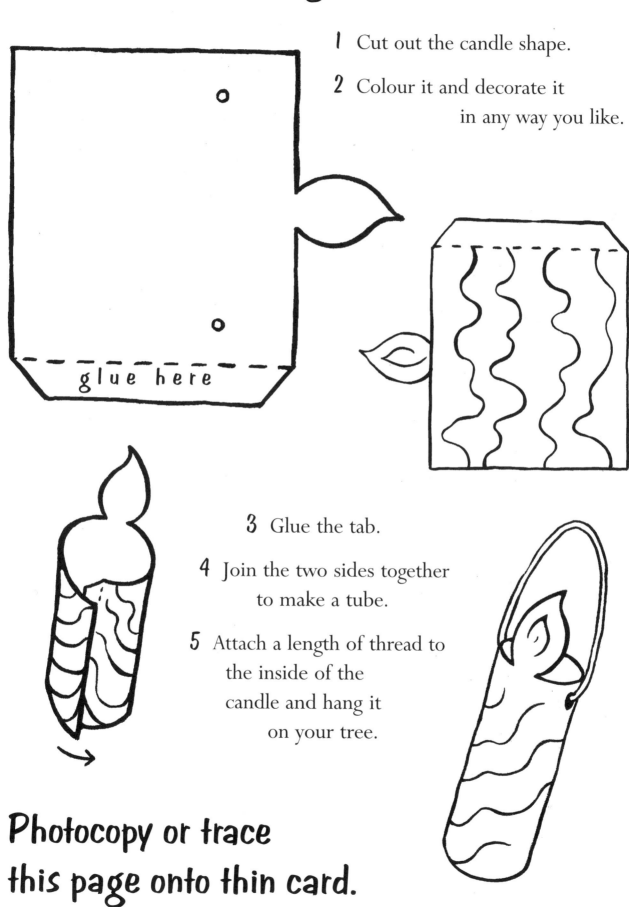

1 Cut out the candle shape.

2 Colour it and decorate it in any way you like.

glue here

3 Glue the tab.

4 Join the two sides together to make a tube.

5 Attach a length of thread to the inside of the candle and hang it on your tree.

Photocopy or trace this page onto thin card.

is for Mary

Mary gave birth to her first-born son, wrapped him in strips of cloth and laid him in a manger.

Luke 2:7

13 December

Have you ever seen a tiny baby? One who is only a few days old? You will know that they are very small and that they need a lot of looking after.

What Mary had been told by the angel Gabriel came true. Her special baby, Jesus, was born and she wrapped him up to keep him safe and warm. She was a long way from her home and her family in Nazareth. The town of Bethlehem was very busy and there was no room for them in the inn; but she did what God had asked her to do—she became the mother of his baby son. Today we still remember Mary for her trust in God and for her obedience.

A prayer for you to use today
Thank you, dear God, for Mary; for her trust, her obedience to you and for the love and care she gave to Jesus, your Son. Amen.

Make this figure of Mary.

1 Cut out the body shape and colour it in.

2 Cut out the arm shapes and colour them in. Bend back on the dotted lines.

3 Glue the card body shape at the tab to form a cone.

4 Cut out the head shape and colour it in. Lay a length of thread on the inside at the dotted line.

5 Fold on the dotted line and run glue around the inside edges of the head shape and hold together until stuck.

6 Slot the arms into the slits in Mary's body and glue the head in place.

7 Tie thread to make a hanger.

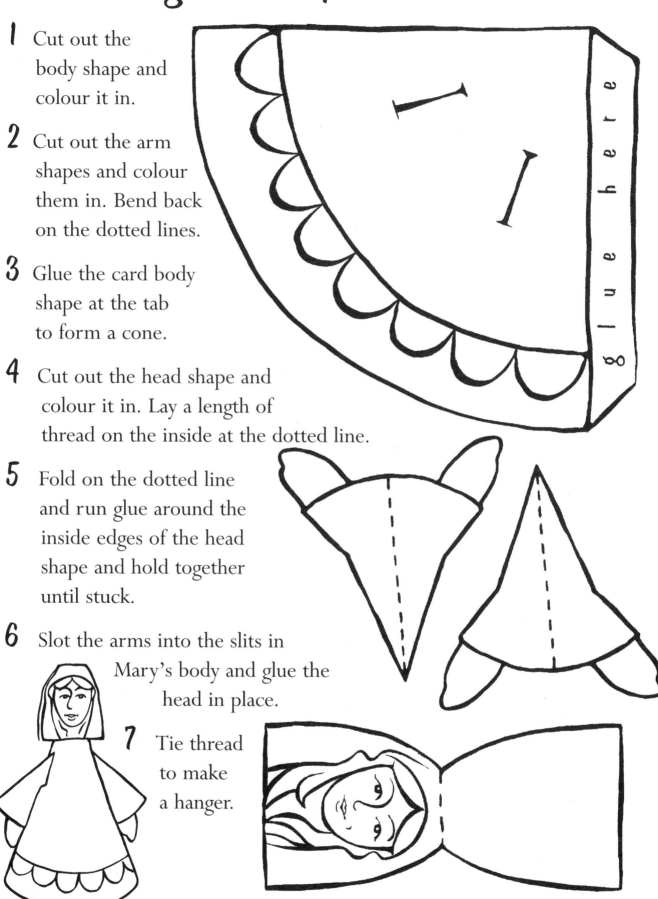

glue here

Photocopy or trace this page onto thin card.

The angel said to them, 'Don't be afraid! I am here with good news for you, which will bring great joy to all the people. This very day in David's town your Saviour was born—Christ the Lord! And this is what will prove it to you: you will find the baby wrapped in strips of cloth and lying in a manger.' Suddenly a great army of heaven's angels appeared with the angel, singing praises to God.

Luke 2:10, 12

is for night

14 December

It was night time, if you remember, when the shepherds were watching their flocks in the fields. They had a visit first from one angel and then from a whole host of God's heavenly angels. We can only imagine the fear and astonishment of the shepherds as the dark night sky lit up with the glory of the angels. One minute they were quietly watching their flocks, the next minute they were in the company of God's messengers, bringing them good news of the birth of a baby. It was all a great surprise.

Can you think of a time when you had a surprise? How did you react?

A prayer for you to use today

Dear heavenly Father, you sent your messenger to the shepherds with the news of the birth of Jesus. Help us to listen to this story and to be as pleased as the shepherds at the birth of Jesus. Amen.

Make a moon mobile to hang on your Christmas tree to remind you it was night when the angels visited the shepherds.

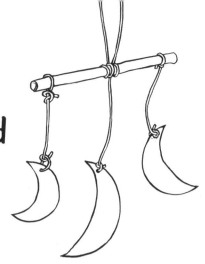

- -

glue here

1 Cut out the moon shapes and colour them on both sides.

2 Make a hole in the top of each one and thread with long lengths of cotton.

3 Cut the template for the stick out of card, and roll up.

4 Hang the moons at different levels along the cylinder.

5 Tie a thread around the centre and, when you are happy with the balance, put small dabs of glue on each thread where it is tied to the stick.

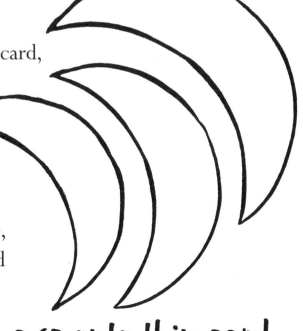

Photocopy or trace this page onto thin card.

When the angels went away from them back into heaven, the shepherds said to one another, 'Let's go to Bethlehem and see this thing that has happened, which the Lord has told us.'

Luke 2:15

is for obey

15 December

I wonder what you would say if you had just had a visit from angels? I think I would want to talk about it. I might wonder if it had been true, if others had seen the same as I did, or if I had imagined it all.

But the shepherds did not stop to think about it or to chat about it all. They obeyed the heavenly vision and left their sheep. They went straight down from the hills to the town of Bethlehem to find what God had told them about.

A prayer for you to use today

Dear God, we might not be visited by angels, but we can read what you have to say to us in your word, the Bible. And we can hear what you have to say to us when other people tell us about you. Help us to listen to you so that we can say 'yes' to you. Amen.

Make a 'yes' bauble for your Christmas tree.

1 Cut out the two circle shapes.

2 Make the cuts where shown.

3 Slot the circles together to see where you need to write the words SAY YES TO GOD. This will fit twice round the bauble.

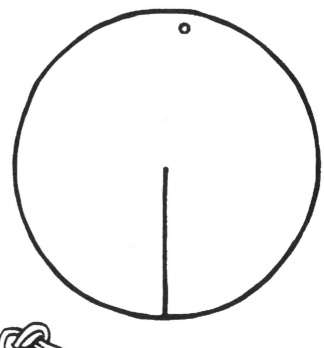

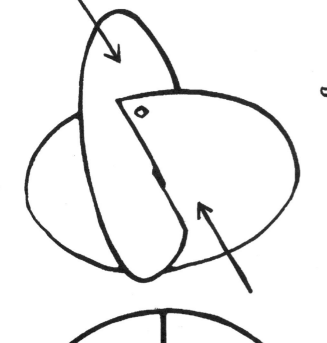

4 Unslot the circles and write the words. Decorate the two halves of your bauble.

5 Slot the two circles together.

6 Make a small hole at the top and thread with cotton to make a hanger.

Photocopy or trace this page onto thin card.

P

*This is what the prophet wrote:
'Bethlehem in the land of Judah, you are
by no means the least of the leading cities of Judah;
for from you will come a leader who
will guide my people Israel.'*

Matthew 2:5–6

is for prophets

16 December

Do you live in a big town or a small village? Perhaps you may even live in a city. If you do, it will be a lot bigger than Bethlehem was at the time when Jesus was born.

A long time before the time of Jesus, holy men of God, called prophets, had written that one day a leader would come to help the Jewish people, the people of Israel. One of these prophets was called Micah and he wrote that this special leader would come from Bethlehem. Bethlehem was very small, but when people were trying to find Jesus, they remembered what Micah had said and it helped them in their search.

A prayer for you to use today
Dear Lord Jesus, we thank you for all the many people all through the ages who have told us about you. We thank you for those who teach us about you today. Amen.

38

Make a scroll like the early prophets wrote upon to hang on your tree.

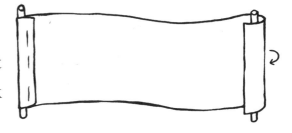

1 Trace and cut two small rectangles out of card. Roll them up tightly and stick where shown to form two tubes.

2 Cut a piece of paper from the long rectangle to make scroll.

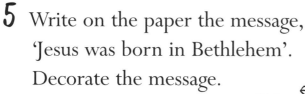

Jesus was born in Bethlehem

3 Roll the end of the paper round the sticks, one at each end of the paper. Glue the paper so that it covers the sticks.

5 Write on the paper the message, 'Jesus was born in Bethlehem'. Decorate the message.

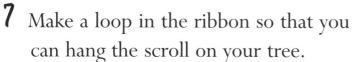

6 Roll up your scroll and tie it with some ribbon.

7 Make a loop in the ribbon so that you can hang the scroll on your tree.

glue here

glue here

glue here

Jesus was born in... Judea, during the time when Herod was king. Soon afterwards, some men who studied the stars came from the east to Jerusalem and asked, 'Where is the baby born to be the king of the Jews? We saw his star when it came up in the east, and we have come to worship him.'

Matthew 2:1–2

Q is for quest

17 December

Have you ever joined in a treasure hunt? If you have, you will know that you have to follow a trail of clues that send you in search of 'the treasure'—but you do not know what that treasure is or where it is until it is found.

The wise men were following the star, but they had no idea where it was taking them. They called on Herod at his palace in Jerusalem, but that was not the right place to find the baby king, so they continued looking carefully wherever they could. We think that they may have travelled for a long time, but they did not give up; they kept on looking.

A prayer for you to use today

O God our Father, you give us lots of ways to know that you are there. We can see you in your world, in all that you have made and we can see you in other people. We thank you for this and ask that we may never be too busy to look for you in everything. Amen.

Make a lantern for your Christmas tree to remind yourself that the wise men travelled by day and night to find Jesus.

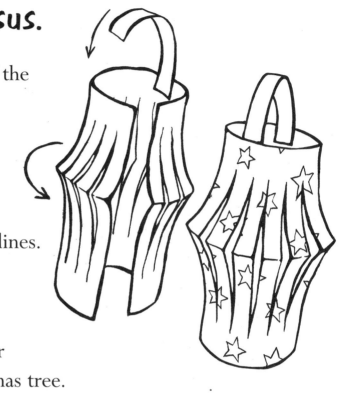

1 Cut out the lantern shape. Cut off the end strip to make the handle.

2 Colour both in and decorate them with gold and silver stars.

3 Fold the lantern in half along the dotted line. Cut along the marked lines.

4 Bend the lantern round and glue the edges together at the tab.

5 Fix the handle over the top of your lantern and hang it on the Christmas tree.

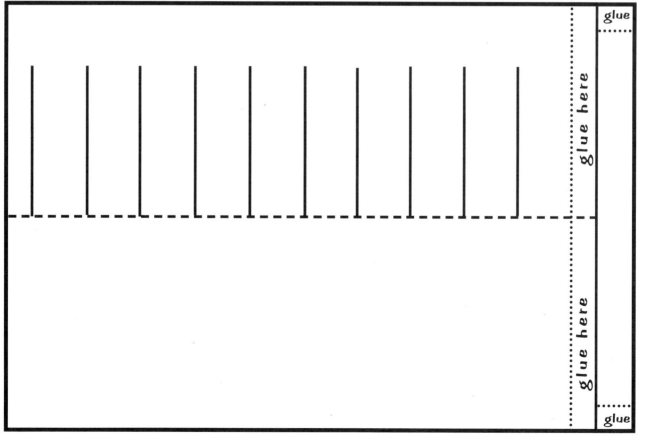

glue

glue here

glue here

glue

Photocopy or trace this page onto thin card.

B is for rushing

So the shepherds hurried off.

Luke 2:16

18 December

Have you ever been so excited to see someone that you have had to run to meet them? The shepherds were like that in our story. After they had seen the vision of angels who told them to go to find the baby, they rushed off as quickly as they could. Perhaps they were so excited that they ran all the way to Bethlehem. They had no idea where they were going but were too happy to worry about that—they just hurried as fast as they could.

A prayer for you to use today

Dear Lord, fill our hearts with such love for you that we can't wait to praise you. Amen.

Make a chain of footsteps to go on your tree.

1 Trace and cut out the footstep shapes as many times as you like.

    2 Colour the shapes.

        3 Make a hole in each end of each foot where marked.

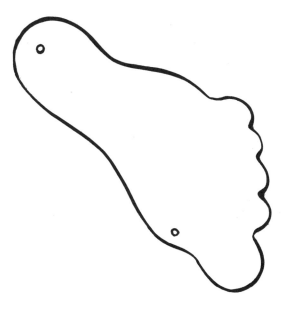

4 String together with cotton thread, tying each one just tight enough for the feet to fit loosely in a long chain, which can be draped on your tree.

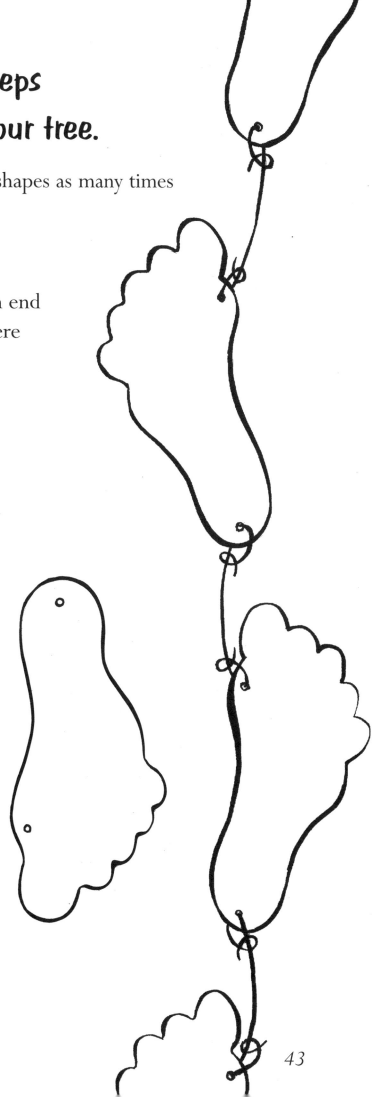

The shepherds found Mary and Joseph, and saw the baby lying in the manger. When the shepherds saw him, they told them what the angel had said about the child.

Luke 2:16–17

is for shepherds

19 December

We have all seen Christmas cards of the shepherds at the stable and it all looks lovely. We must not forget that a stable is where animals live, and so it may have been rather smelly. It might also have been dirty and cold.

The shepherds do not seem to have had any trouble finding where to go. They saw the baby Jesus and they were able to tell Mary and Joseph about the angel's message. How wonderful it was for them to look at this small child and to realize that he was so special.

A prayer for you to use today

Dear Jesus, as we look at you lying in the manger in the stable, please help us to realize how special you are. Help us to also be as pleased as the shepherds were. Amen.

Make these figures of the shepherds.

1 Cut out a body shape for each shepherd and colour them in.

2 Cut out two arm shapes for each shepherd and colour them in. Bend back on the dotted lines.

3 Glue each card body shape at the tab to form a cone.

4 Cut out a head shape for each shepherd and colour them in. Lay a length of thread on the inside of each one at the dotted line.

5 Fold on the dotted line and run glue around the inside edges of the head shape and hold together until stuck.

6 Slot the arms into the slits in each shepherd's body and glue the head in place.

7 Tie the thread to form a hanger.

glue here

Photocopy or trace this page onto thin card.

 **is for treasure**

20 December

Some things are so amazing that we don't always want to talk about them. Sometimes we just want to be quiet and think about something or someone very special. This is what happened to Mary. She remembered what the angel Gabriel had said to her when he came to tell her that she would have a baby. Now the shepherds told her that angels had visited them. What was she to make of it all? Perhaps she did not really understand, but just accepted it as treasure from God to be kept in her heart. The New International Version of the Bible says, 'Mary treasured up all these things and pondered them in her heart.'

A prayer for you to use today

Dear God you give us so much. We thank you especially for those very special moments when all we want to do is to think quietly about the treasures you give us and to save them in our hearts. Amen.

Make a heart to hang on your tree.

1 Cut out the two heart shapes.

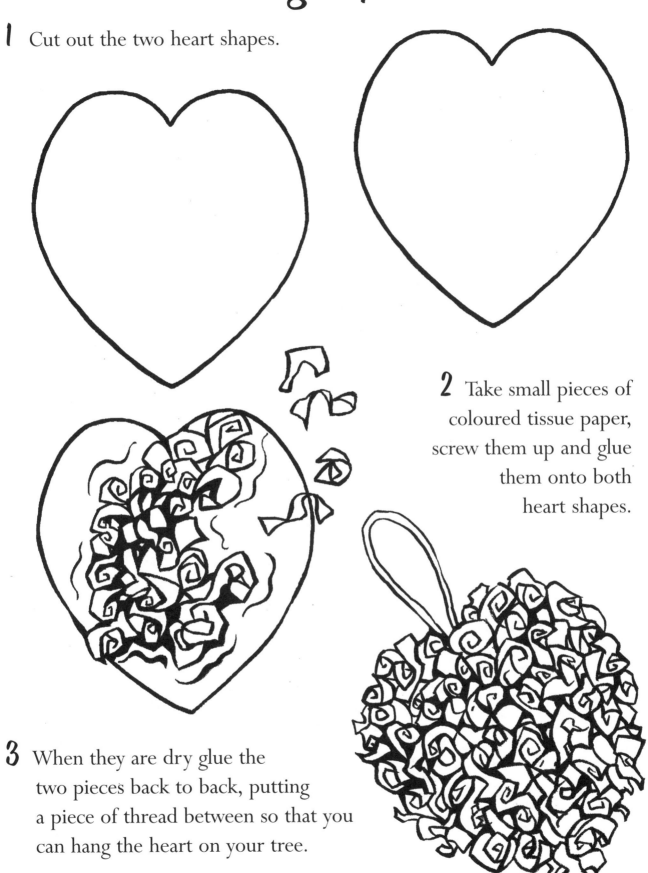

2 Take small pieces of coloured tissue paper, screw them up and glue them onto both heart shapes.

3 When they are dry glue the two pieces back to back, putting a piece of thread between so that you can hang the heart on your tree.

Photocopy or trace this page onto thin card.

On their way the wise men saw the same star they had seen in the east. When they saw it how happy they were, what joy was theirs! It went ahead of them until it stopped over the place where the child was.

Matthew 2:9

u is for under a star

21 December

Have you ever stood under the stars at night? There are more than you could count! If you have ever tried to follow a star you will know how hard it is, because stars are so far away.

The wise men had left their own country to follow a new star that they had noticed in the sky. (They must have known a lot about stars to notice that there was a new one). When they went to Jerusalem and met Herod, they lost sight of the star, but now they could see it again and they were very pleased. They followed it to find out where it led.

A prayer for you to use today
Loving God, we thank you for all the wonderful things you have made. Thank you that you use your creation to tell us about yourself. Help us to look for you in everything around us. Amen.

Make star (or several stars) for your tree.

1 Cut out two star shapes.

2 Colour or cover them with silver or gold paper.

3 Cut the stars where marked.

4 Fit the two pieces together as shown in the diagram

5 Make a hole where shown and tie a thread through to form a hanger.

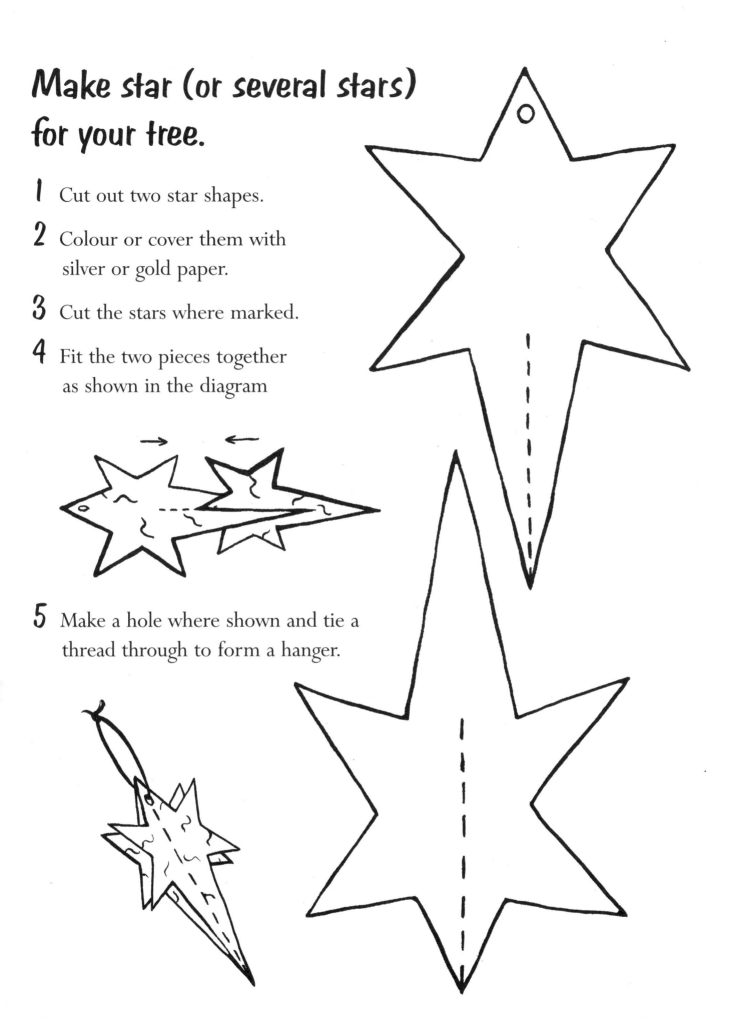

Photocopy or trace this page onto thin card.

The wise men went into the house, and when they saw the child with his mother Mary, they knelt down and worshipped him.

Matthew 2:11

is for visitors

22 December

Do you like having visitors? I expect it depends upon who it is, but most of us like to have people to visit us.

The wise men followed the star and it led them to where Jesus was, and they were able to visit him at last. We do not know how long it took them to get this far. It may be that Jesus was not a tiny baby and it may be that he and Mary and Joseph were no longer in the stable. That does not really matter very much. What matters is that the wise men finally arrived to make their long-planned visit.

A prayer for you to use today

Dear Lord Jesus, as we get very near to Christmas, which is your birthday, help us to think about how we would get ready to welcome you into our homes. And then help us to welcome you into our hearts. Amen.

50

Make these figures of the three wise men.

1 Cut out a body shape for each wise man and colour them in.

2 Cut out two arm shapes for each wise man and colour them in. Bend back on the dotted lines.

3 Glue each card body shape at the tab to form a cone.

4 Cut out a head shape for each wise man and colour them in. Lay a length of thread on the inside of each one at the dotted line.

5 Fold on the dotted line and run glue around the inside edges of the head shape and hold together until stuck.

6 Slot the arms into the slits in each wise man's body and glue the head in place.

7 Tie the thread to form a hanger.

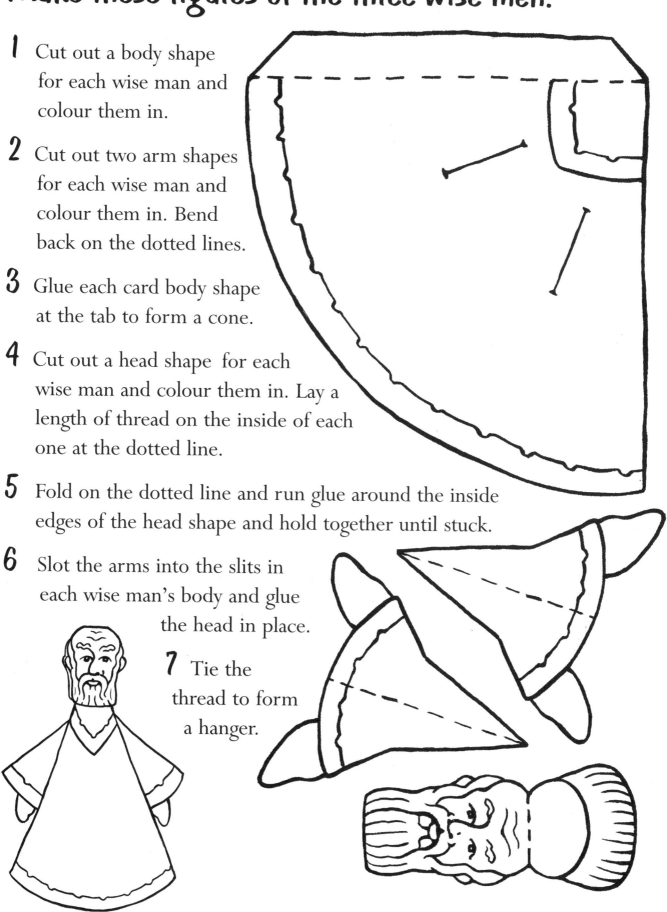

Photocopy or trace this page onto thin card.

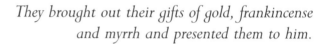

They brought out their gifts of gold, frankincense and myrrh and presented them to him.

Matthew 2:11

W is for the wise men's gifts

23 December

What presents would you give to a baby? A toy? Some clothes? A blanket? I don't expect you would think of giving gold or frankincense or myrrh like the wise men gave to Jesus.

These were very different presents. Gold was the kind of gift that was given to a king (Jesus was called the king of the Jews). Frankincense was sweet smelling and was used in the worship of God (Jesus was God's Son). Myrrh was used when people died (Jesus was to die on the cross when he was grown up). Perhaps they were good presents for the baby Jesus after all.

What present would you like to give to baby Jesus?

A prayer for you to use today
We love you, Lord Jesus. Please accept the gift of our love, which is the best present we can give you for your birthday. Amen.

Make a pyramid of the gifts from the wise men for your tree.

1 Cut out the pyramid shape and colour it in.

2 Colour in the gifts.

3 Make up the pyramid shape by gluing the tab where shown.

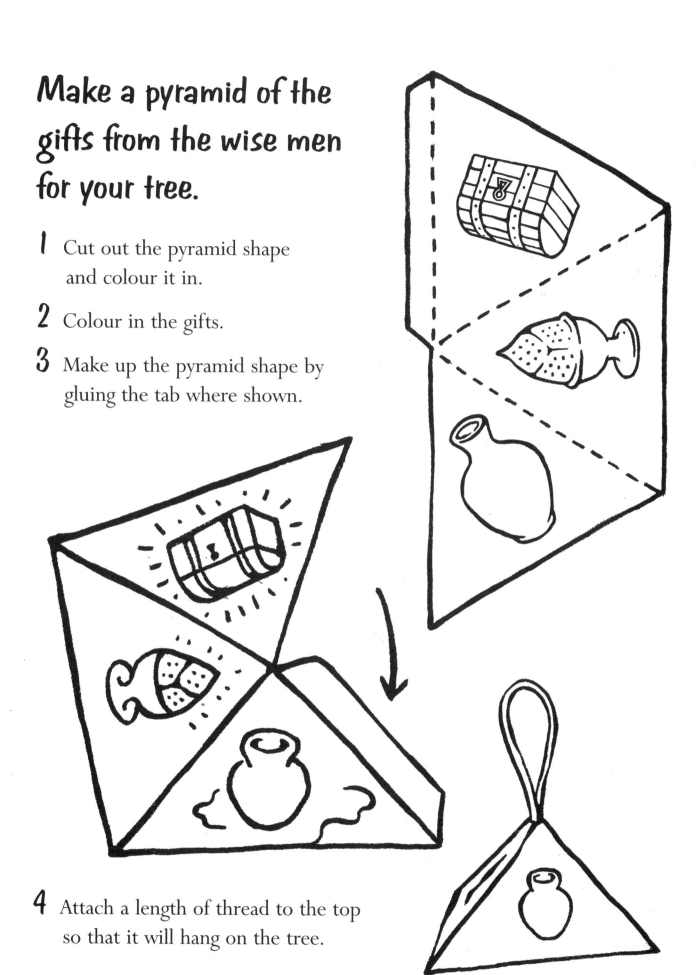

4 Attach a length of thread to the top so that it will hang on the tree.

Photocopy or trace this page onto thin card.

XYZ

are for the love that has no end

He will be great and he will be called the Son of the Most High God... his kingdom will never end!

Luke 1:32–33

24 December

Have you noticed how the story of Christmas is the story of God's love? Mary treasured God's love in her heart. The shepherds ran to Bethlehem when they heard the angel's message. The wise men travelled for a long time following a star just to visit Jesus.

This tiny baby was talked about by the prophets, his birth was announced by angels, he was called Immanuel 'God with us'. He is the Son of the Most High God, and his love for us has no beginning and no end—it is always there.

As we come to Christmas Day we too can kneel down and worship him— that baby wrapped up and lying in a manger; that baby who is the Son of God.

A prayer for you to use today

Happy Birthday Jesus. Help me to show you that I love you by loving others. Amen.

On this very special night ask a grown up if they will help you to light a candle and stand it in the window of your house to show your love for Jesus.

54

To finish your Christmas tree, make the baby in the manger.

1 Cut out the baby and the manger and colour in.

2 Fold dotted lines on manger and glue tabs into place. Make holes in straw where shown. Roll the figure of the baby and insert tabs into the holes. Glue in place. Glue straw onto manger.

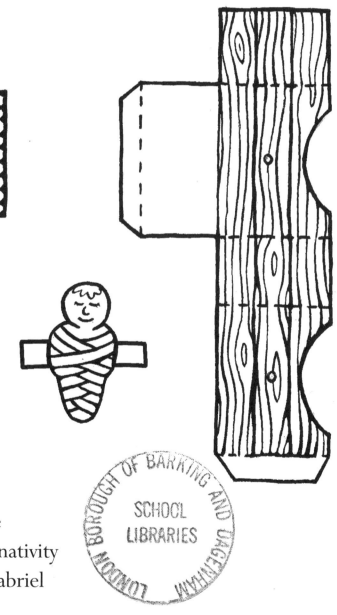

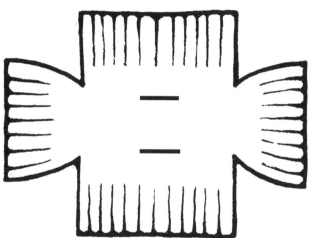

3 Make holes in side of manger where shown.

4 Thread a length of cotton through holes to form hanger. You can hang all your special figures—Jesus in the manger, Mary, Joseph, the shepherds and wise men—together on the front of your tree, to make the nativity scene. You can add the angel Gabriel and the star if you want to.

Photocopy or trace this page onto thin card.

Published by
The Bible Reading Fellowship
Ist Floor, Elsfield Hall,
15–17 Elsfield Way, Oxford OX2 5FG

ISBN 0 7459 3553 2

First published 1997
10 9 8 7 6 5 4 3 2 1

Acknowledgments
Scripture quotations are taken from the Good News Bible
published by The Bible Societies/HarperCollins Publishers Ltd, UK
© American Bible Society 1966, 1971, 1976, 1992, used with permission.

A catalogue record for this book is available
from the British Library

Printed and bound in Malta
by Interprint Ltd